THE
NIGER

AFRICA'S RIVER
OF MYSTERY

by JANE WERNER WATSON

Maps by Henri Fluchere

GARRARD PUBLISHING COMPANY
CHAMPAIGN, ILLINOIS

Contents

This scene on the banks of the smooth-flowing Niger is framed
by the twisting roots of a baobab tree.

1. An Easy Task

Today when we want to learn about the Niger River, we have an easy task. We can look at a map of West Africa, like the one on the following pages. There we can quickly trace with a finger the river's 2,600-mile course.

We may be surprised to see that the Niger starts less than 200 miles inland from the coastline of Africa's western bulge. It may seem strange that the river flows north almost to the sands of the Sahara before swinging around in a wide arc to head southward for the Gulf of Guinea. We may be surprised, but we see no mystery here.

For more than two thousand years, though, the Niger was Africa's river of mystery. Greeks and Romans of

West Africa

MAURITANIA

S A H A R A

Nile River

A F R I C A

Niger River

Congo River

Timbuktu

Senegal River

SENEGAL

M A L I

Dakar

Inland Delta

Sansanding

Mopti

Gambia River

Koulikoro

Djenne

GAMBIA

Bamako

Niger River

Bani River

PORTUGUESE GUINEA

UPPER

GUINEA

Atlantic Ocean

SIERRA LEONE

IVORY COAST

LIBERIA

Gulf of

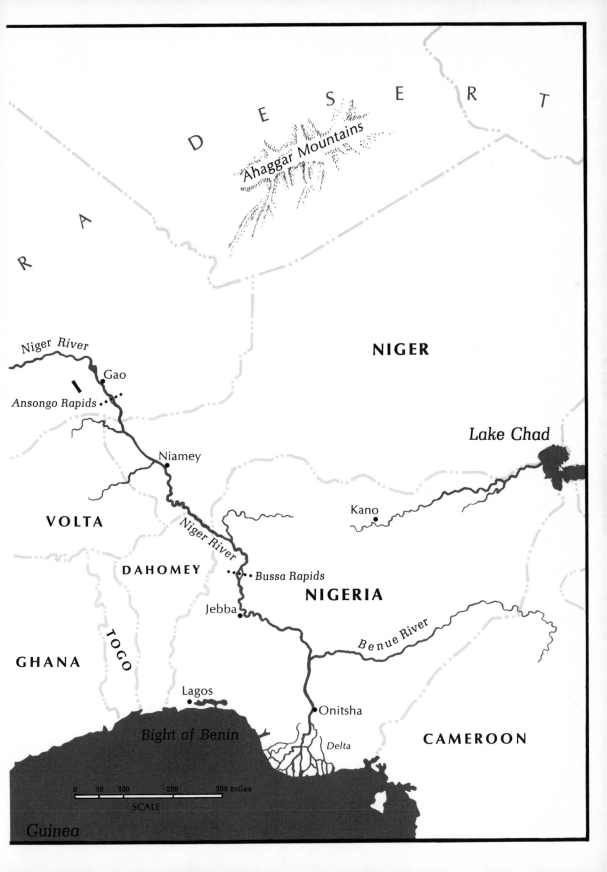

Wild animals used to roam freely over the grasslands. Today elephants like these are seen only in game preserves.

ancient times had heard tales of such a river, but less than a century ago its whole course was still not known. Almost until that time, geographers were arguing as to where—or if—the Niger flowed into the sea.

Scores of explorers and their parties died trying to trace the river's course, but still its mystery lured men. They traveled across burning deserts, through dripping rain forests and dry bush country, by camel, horse, and dugout canoe.

Wherever the explorers went, they found Africans of the Niger basin living in well-established villages and towns. They saw well-tended farms, fleets of fishing boats, and busy marketplaces.

Explorers also found elephants, shy antelopes, even an occasional leopard at home on the grasslands. Flamingos, kingfishers, geese, and other water birds gathered in flocks on quiet stretches of the river. Great gray hippopotamuses wallowed in shallow pools, as they still do today, raising their heads in gigantic pink yawns.

One expects to find wild animals in Africa, of course. More surprising to most people is to learn that, along the grasslands of the northern curve of the Niger, great nations and empires prospered for a thousand years.

A herd of hippopotamuses enjoy their morning swim.

These kingdoms were little known beyond West Africa. A desert to the north and rain forests to the south shut them away from most of the world.

In spite of these barriers, the Niger basin has never been really isolated. Even in early times some hardy Negroes did travel across the desert. For many centuries the ancestors of today's peoples of the Niger moved about on the grasslands in large family and tribal groups. Some groups traveled southeastward through the rain forests and can be found today throughout the southern half of Africa. Others were taken as slaves to North and South America and to the West Indies, after European traders found their way to West Africa. So Niger-basin ways of living and traditions spread to many lands.

Then came European soldiers, and for most of a century governments of Europe ruled West Africa. Today there are again independent nations along the Niger: Guinea, Mali, Niger, and Nigeria. They and their friendly people are still relatively little known to outsiders. Today, however, one can visit these nations easily by airplane and car—and in the pages of this book.

2. Great Kingdoms of the Past

Lines of men marched wearily across a stony wasteland that seemed endless. They were crossing the great African Sahara and were bound for a market town in the far-off green land along the Mediterranean Sea.

Sturdy, dark-skinned men like these had made the long march across the Sahara for many hundreds of years. Their homes were in the grasslands that stretch along the curve of the Niger and most of the way across Africa, south of the desert. These men carried the riches of the grasslands north to sell in Mediterranean market towns.

Some carried patterned hides of antelope and leopard.

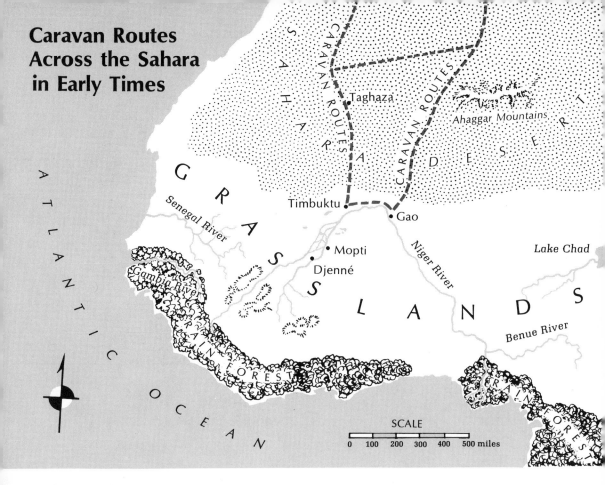

Caravan Routes Across the Sahara in Early Times

Taghaza

Ahaggar Mountains

CARAVAN ROUTES

CARAVAN ROUTES

S A H A R A   D E S E R T

G R A S S L A N D S

Senegal River

Gambia River

Timbuktu

Gao

Mopti

Djenné

Niger River

Lake Chad

Benue River

ATLANTIC OCEAN

RAIN FOREST

RAIN FOREST

SCALE
0   100   200   300   400   500 miles

Others balanced on their heads long curving ivory tusks of grassland elephants. Still others had bundles of feathery ostrich plumes, each plume as long as a man's forearm. There was a market for all these goods, but the men of the north liked best to trade for gold. Knowing this, the grassland men carried small sacks of bright golden grains and nuggets along with their furs and feathers and ivory.

North African traders had often wondered about the lands that could provide all these riches. Men of the grasslands told them that the gold was found among the stones in riverbeds. They also told about the great river that watered grassland fields and carried boats from town to town.

North African traders were not especially interested in tales of the great river. What they wanted was the gold and ivory. Whenever any of them started south, however, the desert stopped them. The sun burned them by day, cold chilled them by night, and the wind blew sharp sand grains into their mouths and eyes. The need to travel across the Sahara slowly and painfully on foot kept men of the north from visiting the grasslands for many hundreds of years.

In the middle of the seventh century, warriors from the desert of Arabia swept across North Africa. They came to conquer lands in order to spread a new religion taught by the prophet Mohammed. They brought more than a new religion, though. Among other things, they brought knowledge of how to live and travel on a desert.

Men of Arabia knew that camels could make desert

Long caravans of camels still plod across the Sahara Desert to Timbuktu carrying slabs of salt. From Timbuktu the slabs are transported by canoe down the Niger to Mopti, below.

travel practical. The first of these "ships of the desert" had been brought into Africa from Asia about A.D. 300, but men from Arabia were the ones who took camels across North Africa in large numbers.

Broad, padded feet gave camels firm footing on sand, and these animals could go for days without water. With camels to ride, the pale-skinned men from North Africa ventured to cross the desert at last, traveling in groups called caravans. For the first time the northerners saw for themselves the rich grasslands on the border of the Sahara.

The most important product these caravans carried south was salt. Until just a few years ago, when trucks in large numbers began to cross the Sahara, salt caravans of 600 to 1,000 camels and 300 to 500 men used to cross the desert regularly. Some still do.

When caravans traveled north, the camels were often loaded with ivory and furs, but the traders also were sure to carry small sacks of precious gold. The best gold, it was said, came from a town twelve miles from "the great river." This fact was reported in a geography book called *Roads and Kingdoms* written by an Arabic traveler in 1067.

The Arabic word for "great river" is "nile." Word of a great river in the grasslands naturally led people to think that this river must be the same as the Nile of Egypt, whose upper reaches were not known.

The next mention of the "nile" of the grasslands in writing was by a North African named Ibn Battuta. He was a great traveler and had wandered across much of the world the Arabs had conquered. In 1352 Ibn Battuta crossed the Sahara to visit the grasslands. There he was invited to appear at the court of a great kingdom of the grasslands and to meet its dark-skinned ruler, the *mansa* of Mali.

The mansa received visitors in a silk pavilion set up in a tree-shaded courtyard of his palace grounds. Around his throne stood 300 slaves and many musicians with drums and horns.

The mansa himself was richly dressed and wore a skullcap of gold. The warriors attending him had swords, and quivers for their arrows, trimmed with gold. The rich saddles and bridles of the royal horses were ornamented with gold.

Like the kings of other African peoples, the mansa was considered sacred, almost a god, as pharaohs had been in ancient Egypt. A sacred king could not be seen eating or drinking like common folk. He could not even speak directly to common people. He always spoke through an interpreter, who was an honored person at the court.

Another honored person was the poet or praise singer. He often wore a special costume topped with a wooden mask to set him apart from other men. The poet recited the list of kings of the past and their adventures.

This present-day king in West Africa is honored by his subjects as was the *mansa* of Mali. He is announced by a royal trumpeter.

In this small village near the Niger River women still pound grain
smooth in the same way their ancestors did.

This king list made up the history of the people and was highly valued.

Ibn Battuta was impressed by the court of the mansa of Mali. He was even more impressed when he traveled about the wide countryside along the great river. The roads were pleasant, shaded with many thick-barreled baobab trees. Best of all, wherever he wandered, the visitor found that he was perfectly safe. There was no robbery in Mali, and the mansa punished any sign of injustice harshly.

A traveler could always buy food from market women in the villages, but Ibn Battuta did not care much for the favorite dish of the people of Mali. It was grain pounded and mixed with honey and milk. This is still a favorite dish today. There was plenty of mutton, though, and good watermelons were available. The melons were grown in the shade of palm trees and on damp riverbanks.

All a traveler really had to carry with him were some small lumps of salt to use as money. The grassland people could produce most of what they needed. Salt they had to import. They valued it so highly that they used some of it as money.

The mansas of Mali and their officials kept the peace in the grasslands and made the roads safe for trade and travel. In return they collected tribute in salt or gold from all caravans, and from every lesser ruler for hundreds of miles around.

Gold for tribute was found in the beds of many of the streams that flowed into the Niger. Women shook sand from the stream bed back and forth in large shallow bowls—as they still do today. Often they found some grains of gold, or even a nugget, in the sand. All nuggets belonged to the ruler. The people could keep gold dust for themselves.

Salt for trade and tribute came from the desert town of Taghaza, far to the north of Mali. Men dug it in squared slabs from under the surface of the earth. Even the houses and mosques of Taghaza were built of blocks of salt.

A camel could carry two of these great flat salt blocks at a time. They brought a high price in gold in the cities of Mali. Three-quarters of this price went to the men of the caravans for making the long and difficult trip across the desert.

The men who ran the caravan trade were mostly

When the religion of Moslem traders started to flourish in the grasslands, mosques like this one near Mopti were built.

North Africans. They did not just barter one kind of goods for another. They used coinage and a system of credit, which were new ideas to the trading people of the grasslands. They found these methods useful and adopted them. Also, the northerners were Moslems who wanted to spread their religion and to trade with other Moslems. So the grassland traders and rulers accepted the new religion too.

Trade prospered, and the kingdom of Mali prospered along the northern curve of the Niger for more than 200 years. Then in the late 1300s, as the rulers of Mali weakened, another people began to rise to power. These were the Songhai.

3. A River of Trade

Songhai poets liked to tell of long-ago times when their people had lived in an ancient city on a river in the land of Misr—the Arabic name for Egypt.

Legend said the Songhai had been in Egypt when Moses was struggling to free his people from the pharaoh—about 1300 B.C. According to this story, the pharaoh sent to the ruler of the Songhai for aid against the plagues caused by Moses' magic.

It was 2,000 years later that the Arabs conquered Egypt and pushed southward, up the Nile. It was probably this invasion that sent the Songhai fleeing westward from upper (southern) Egypt. Historians think the Songhai probably spent more than 100 years on the move. They stopped along the way frequently to grow crops, but not until they reached a river like the Nile did they really settle down.

There on the bank of the Niger the Songhai founded a city called Gao. It became their capital. Some of the people continued westward to the low country where the river spreads out into a network of streams and channels. Along the Bani, largest tributary of the upper Niger, these channels cut the low land into many small islands. On one of these islands the Songhai founded the town of Djenné (Jen-*nay*).

As the Songhai empire grew strong, it expanded into land held by the Mali empire and began to rule the people of Mali.

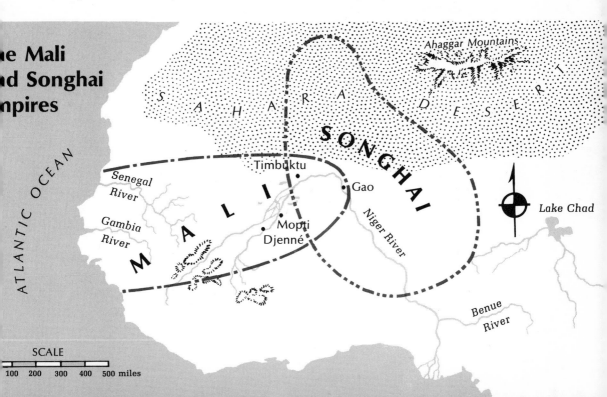

Djenné, ancient city of the Songhai empire, today. The river is seen curving around the city at the upper left.

Even today visitors have to reach Djenné by boat. The river channels on all sides form a protective moat around the city. At low water, it is true that enemies could ford the river, but they would have to do so under the eyes of armed warriors of Djenné. When water in the river is low, the banks are high and slippery. Invaders would have to climb these steep mud banks under a rain of spears and arrows. With these protections, it is not surprising that Djenné, though it was besieged, was never really invaded by enemies.

Old tales tell that the rulers of Djenné used to control 7,000 villages. The rulers' commands were called out from the gate of the city. All the villages were so close together along the network of waterways that orders could be swiftly passed along by voice to the farthest village.

These villages and the city of Djenné became part of the great Songhai empire as it spread out from Gao. From the mid-1400s until about 1600, the Songhai people ruled most of the area that Mali had dominated earlier. The Songhai controlled the desert as far north as the salt mines. Their power was felt as far west as the Atlantic and as far east as Lake Chad. They boasted that it took six months to cross Songhai territory.

During the great days of the Songhai empire, all this land was ruled by viceroys and provincial governors. There was a large standing army of cavalry and foot soldiers. There was a navy on the Niger. Together these forces kept the empire safe for trade. Canals were dug to lead river water to fields, so there was plenty of water to grow food. Farmers shared in the country's prosperity.

Many villagers lived in the wooded hills to the south. Traders of Djenné bought fruits and kola nuts, furs and bundles of wood from these forest villagers. The traders then loaded their purchases on canoes and shipped them downriver.

Some traders shipped boatloads of goods to branch offices they had set up along the Niger in cities like Mopti and Timbuktu. Others had traveling salesmen who received a share of all the goods or money they took in trade. We would say today that they worked on commission.

The traders of Djenné were good businessmen, and they were also known as kindly and good-natured men.

Young traders carried their goods down the Niger River in boats that looked much like these present-day craft.

If a young man wanted to go into business for himself, but did not have money to buy a boatload of fruit, furs, and river fish, a trader of Djenné would let him take the goods on credit. When they were sold, the young man would come back with a boatload of salt, cloth, beads, copper, and cowrie shells. He would repay the trader who had trusted him and have some goods to sell on his own.

Boats built for this trade on the Bani and the Niger were often as much as sixty feet long and ten feet wide. They were made of blocks of ebony and cedarwood.

Huge canopied boats still line the shores of the Niger at the busy market town of Mopti.

The blocks were held firmly together with bands of rope, perhaps made from the fibrous bark of the baobab tree. They were chinked with clay, straw, and hemp to make them watertight.

These boats carried passengers as well as freight. To shelter the passengers, an awning of straw arched above the boat amidships. Passengers often paid for their passage in cowrie shells.

Some of these passengers traveled only as far as Mopti. Mopti stands at the junction of the Bani and Niger rivers. Its mud-plastered buildings are scattered over three islands joined by long causeways. The city is still a busy port for riverboats.

Other passengers continued downstream for about 200 miles beyond Mopti. This seven-day journey took them to Timbuktu. When Ibn Battuta visited Timbuktu in 1352, it was known as "the city where canoes and caravans meet." Ever since those days, its name has lured travelers like the sound of distant drums. Timbuktu is worth a closer look.

4. The Roads to Timbuktu

The Niger near Timbuktu did not look like a great trade route in 1352, and it does not today. Along the flat stretch from Mopti to Timbuktu, highland streams have deposited their loads of mud and silt for ages. These deposits have built up an inland delta much like the deltas other great rivers have built at their mouths.

As deposits of mud piled up, the slow-moving waters have been pushed this way and that by the heaps of earth, to form many channels. Reeds and other plants have grown up in the mud, so that small craft travel between walls of tall grasses, over a surface bright with water lilies.

A cluster of large lakes is scattered through this

marshy country. In the winters huge flocks of ducks fly to the warm waters from distant Europe and Asia. As boats approach this area, water birds large and small fly up from their nesting spots.

This marshy country extends up to the edge of the desert, so desert nomads have long wandered here with their flocks. About A.D. 1200, some of the wandering Tuareg people found a place where it was easy to dig wells. They set up a fixed camp of straw huts hedged with thornbushes there on the bank of a stream. The camp was just a few miles from the main channel of the Niger.

Traders from Djenné soon found this camp a convenient place to beach their canoes when they came north to meet salt caravans. They taught the people to make sun-dried brick, which was better suited to permanent homes than straw. The traders also built a warehouse where travelers could leave their goods. The old slave woman who looked after the warehouse was called "the ancient one," or, in the local language, "Timbuktu." From her the settlement got its name, it is said.

Soon caravans from Egypt, from Fez in Morocco, from Gadàmes in Libya wound their way down the

The ancient city of Timbuktu

long desert tracks to Timbuktu. In 1335 the capital of Mali was moved here. The mansas ruled from a now-vanished palace until 1433. Then nomadic Tuaregs from the desert swept in and took the city. In 1469 the Songhai soldier king, Sunni Ali, captured Timbuktu. For more than a century after that, it was one of the principal cities of an empire even wider than Mali had been.

In 1513 another traveler-writer, a Spanish Moor named Leo Africanus, visited the city and wrote about it admiringly. Thanks to him, we know a good deal about life in Timbuktu during its great days.

A canal had been dug from the main channel of the Niger through the marsh to Timbuktu. This meant that, even when the river was low, canoes could reach the city. From the head of the canal, cargoes of hides, grain, musk, ostrich plumes, gold, and ivory were carried into town on the backs of donkeys.

The skyline of the town was dominated by the pointed towers of great mud-walled mosques. Around them rose thick-walled houses, two and three stories tall. Along the narrow, sunbaked streets there were countless workshops where skilled craftsmen worked at weaving, metalsmithing, and other trades. Many merchants lived in fine homes above their shops or storerooms.

Timbuktu was rich in learning as well as in trade. There were many schools. In cool, dim, upper rooms scholars sat reading, writing, and discussing thick books handwritten in the fine Arabic script.

Rich merchants and scholars lived well in Timbuktu. They ate from handsome trays and bowls of tinned brass. These, along with rich brocades for the men's robes, had been carried down by camel from Morocco.

The wives of rich merchants, scholars, and men of the court had servants to care for their homes and children. This gave the ladies plenty of time to make themselves beautiful. They stained their nails with henna and outlined their eyes with coal-black antimony. They wound pearls and sequins in their black hair and hung jewelry on their arms and necks. In the cool of thick-walled rooms they liked to sit on rich carpets, visiting with friends. Sometimes one of them played on a one-stringed instrument.

At midday the people of Timbuktu ate their main meal of mutton, *kouskous* (a porridge made of grain), biscuits, and honey cakes. They enjoyed sugar, salt, and dates, all brought from the north. They liked sweet, hot tea to drink.

In the cool of the evenings, people ventured out of their houses. Then the streets were lively with groups visiting, listening to music, or dancing.

The rich merchants and scholars of Timbuktu have vanished, along with the wealth of the city. Only about

In the shade of a baobab tree, this Moslem reads a book written in Arabic script as in the days of the Songhai empire.

These Tuareg men, traveling across the desert, veil their faces against the windblown sands of the Sahara.

9,000 persons live there today, and the once busy streets are adrift with desert sand. The once handsome houses with their carved doors and shuttered windows are now worn by the rains and wind-driven sands of centuries and cracked by the heat of the desert sun.

What happened to Timbuktu followed the pattern of the rise and fall of great nations all over the world. By the late 1500s, the Songhai kings were weakening. In the north, the Moors, greedy for the wealth of the grassland empire, decided to invade.

The fact that the Moors had gunpowder, muskets, and cannons decided the contest in their favor. Confronted by these dreadful killing machines, the Songhai warriors lost battle after battle and finally surrendered.

Timbuktu was conquered in 1591, and by 1595 the conquest of the Songhai empire was complete. Most of the victorious Moors were not interested in staying in the hot grasslands, however. So their conquest was short-lived. Tuaregs from the desert soon began once again to raid the cities along the Niger.

These tall, sturdy nomads were skillful hunters and hard fighters. By 1800 they controlled, in a rough sort of way, Timbuktu, Gao, and most of the surrounding

Niger country. The Tuaregs destroyed farms to make more grazing land for their herds. They terrified the city people, kidnapping many to sell them into slavery. They robbed or overcharged traders until the traders stopped coming, and the markets were soon empty.

The Tuaregs were able fighters, but they were not strong rulers. Other desert tribes, called the Foulbes, soon took over from them. These Foulbes detested Europeans, so the curve of the Niger became especially dangerous country for Europeans.

Dangerous or not, this little known part of Africa drew brave explorers. There were many men who longed to solve the mystery of the Niger. The one who was to become most famous for his efforts was a young Scottish doctor named Mungo Park.

5. Journey to the End of the World

Mungo Park first landed in Africa, at the mouth of the Gambia River on the west coast, in 1795. He had been hired by a group of Englishmen who called themselves the Association for Promoting the Discovery of the Inland Parts of Africa. The mission of the young Scottish physician, who was only twenty-four, was to find the course, rise, and termination of the Niger and to visit the principal river towns. The association hoped to add to men's knowledge of the world. It also had a sharp eye for possible routes for profitable trade.

There were many opinions on the course of the Niger. An Arab geographer, Idrisi, back in the twelfth century, had decided that it flowed to the west. He said that in the Mountains of the Moon there were springs —he called them fountains—from which flowed two streams. One became the Nile of Egypt, flowing northward; the other, said Idrisi, flowed westward through great lakes to form the Nile of the Negroes. Roman geographers 1,000 years before had already spoken of this river as Nigris or Nigir.

In Mungo Park's day the Mountains of the Moon, which rise in Uganda, had not yet been explored. Today these mountains are known as the Ruwenzori. The Nile of Egypt had not yet been traced to its source, but the source actually is, as Idrisi said, very close to these mountains.

In the 1440s European explorers, sent by Prince Henry the Navigator of Portugal, sailed along Africa's west coast. Upon finding the mouth of a large river flowing into the Atlantic, they assumed it to be the mouth of the Nile of the Negroes described by Idrisi. They were mistaken, of course. The river they had found was the Senegal, and their error added further to the confusion about the Niger.

Perhaps this misleading report from the Portuguese sailors influenced Leo Africanus, the sixteenth-century geographer. He had actually seen the Niger close to Timbuktu, but he continued to think it flowed west to the Atlantic. Map makers of his time went on showing it this way. In Africa some said simply that the Niger flowed "to the end of the world."

Mungo Park determined to find out the truth. He started his journey by traveling up the Gambia River. After a visit with an English trader, he started overland on horseback, accompanied only by two servants on donkeys. They had no extra animals to carry supplies, so they traveled very light.

They took along some beads, amber, and tobacco for trading. Dr. Park had a pocket sextant and compass to find directions. He carried shotguns and pistols for protection and for hunting food. He also had a thermometer, an umbrella, and a few extra clothes. For safekeeping he tucked the notes he wrote about the journey into the inner band of his hat.

Unfortunately this was not a peaceful period on the grasslands. There were no strong rulers to keep the trade routes safe for travelers. Instead each local chieftain demanded a toll from strangers crossing his land. One Moorish chieftain even imprisoned Mungo Park as

Mungo Park, at left, risked his life to explore the mysterious Niger. Below, is an illustration from his book showing Park's men crossing a stream on a bamboo bridge.

a spy. Park escaped with his life, but he lost all his supplies.

What saved Mungo Park as he traveled on was the kindness of women in many villages. Repeatedly they gave him fish and meal to eat and found him shelter and a sleeping mat at night. Occasionally, too, a friendly king gave the traveler a sack of cowrie shells, useful in buying food.

Finally a bright day came. "I saw with infinite pleasure the great object of my mission," Mungo Park wrote. It was "the long sought-for majestic Niger, glittering in the morning sun, as broad as the Thames at Westminster, and flowing slowly *to the eastward.*"

Mungo Park was the first European to explore the Niger. His exploration solved one of the mysteries of the river. He had seen for himself that it flowed not westward toward the Atlantic, but eastward to some unknown goal.

When Dr. Park took a boat downstream (from a town near Bamako), he was surprised to find some well cultivated fields along the river. Dotted among them were towns with towers of Moslem mosques rising above the low walls. He was surprised, too, to find that many of the people he met feared him. He did not know that most Negro peoples picture the devil as having white skin.

People also thought the young stranger possessed magic, because they saw him writing. Any written word, he discovered, was considered magic. Perhaps the reason was that Moslems often carried bits of holy writing in small cases around their necks to bring them luck and strength. Mungo Park was often asked to write "charms" like this for people he met. He wrote for them the Lord's Prayer of his faith.

Time passed slowly for the lone traveler. The heat of the days, the damp chill of the nights, and the attacks of hordes of mosquitoes gradually took their toll of the young man's strength. In addition, the villagers along the way had little food, even for themselves. They had less to give away. There was also danger from unfriendly rulers. At last Mungo Park realized he could go no farther alone.

Weak and hungry and with only rags left of his clothes, he fell ill of one of the fevers that plagued Europeans in Africa. Kindly Negroes tended him for months, until he gathered strength. Then he made his

Park and his men visited villages of round grass-roofed houses, above, like the present-day village of Jebba, below, on the Niger.

way back to the Atlantic, traveling with a slave cara-van, called a coffle. At the coast he obtained passage as surgeon on a slave ship bound for the West Indies. From there he finally reached his home in Scotland.

Working from the notes he had carried in his hat band and from memory, Mungo Park wrote a book called *Travels in the Interior of Africa*, which is still exciting to read today. He married and settled down to the life of a country doctor in Scotland. The lure of Africa was in his blood, though, and made his long daily round seem very dull.

In 1803 the British government invited him to return to the Niger. This time he was to head a properly outfitted expedition. He was to have plenty of gifts for the local rulers and money to buy and equip two large canoes. His wife and babies were assured of an income if he did not return.

Dr. Park gladly accepted the leadership of the new expedition. He said his farewells and, taking his young brother-in-law as his second-in-command, departed again for Africa.

Nearly forty people started inland from the west coast. The party included a map maker, several skilled workmen, two sailors, and some soldiers. The journey promised to be much more pleasant than Park's earlier, lonely one. However, inland Africa seemed to resist being explored.

Fever and trouble with local rulers soon laid a heavy hand on the party. By the time it reached the Niger, only eleven of the Europeans were still alive.

Those who remained took canoes at the village of Bamako. The party passed through the rapids that make the shallow river dangerous below Bamako. When the explorers reached Sansanding, they were told that the river would provide smooth travel for hundreds of miles. The local ruler gave Dr. Park permission to explore downstream, so he set out to buy a suitable big boat. All that were offered to him, alas, were canoes whose wood was rotting into holes.

There was no choice. Mungo Park bought two of the rotting canoes and started piecing their sound halves together. Only one of his soldiers was strong enough to help him with the task, but at last it was completed. The result was a canoe, forty feet long and six feet wide, that drew only a foot of water. Park named it the *Joliba*—the local name of the Niger River.

Africans still travel in dugout canoes like those Park patched together for his journey down the Niger.

It was mid-November of 1805 when Mungo Park loaded his sickly crew aboard and started downriver again. The draftsman who was to have mapped the river was dead by this time. So were Park's young brother-in-law, all the skilled workmen, and most of the soldiers. The prospects were gloomy. However, Mungo Park wrote home that he planned to continue without stopping until he reached the coast. He expected to do this by the end of January 1806.

He also wrote to the men in the Colonial Office who had planned the expedition. "I shall set sail for the east," he said, "with the fixed resolution to discover the termination of the Niger or perish in the attempt."

Park entrusted these letters to a Negro guide, Isaaco by name, who carried them back to the Gambia. The letters reached England in due time—the last word that was ever received from Mungo Park.

After some months word drifted back to the trading stations on the Gambia that disaster had overtaken the *Joliba* and its crew. The British hired the guide, Isaaco, to return to the spot where he had left the party and to search for news of Park. This was what he learned.

The *Joliba*, well stocked with food, guns, and ammunition, had kept to the Niger for 1,000 miles. Isaaco traced the boat's progress through the confusing maze of swamps and past the river harbor of Timbuktu. He learned that the sturdy craft had made its way past the old city of Gao. It had dodged rocks and rapids and fought off parties of hostile river men.

The *Joliba* had reached the great bend of the Niger, where rocky outcroppings force the river to turn southward. From this point on, dangerous rocks and rapids increased. The small party passed the rocky bars of Ansongo that stop most boats. They made their way through what one traveler described later as "a hopeless labyrinth of rocks, islands, reefs and rapids." The *Joliba* was well beyond the end of the 1,057 miles of the middle river that are considered safe for navigation today. Then, on the rocks of the narrow and dangerous Bussa Rapids, the boat stuck fast.

No efforts could free it. As Park and his one remaining officer worked feverishly, a hostile crowd, armed with bows and arrows and spears, appeared on the shore. The weakened party could not fight off the attack for long. The boat began to break up.

Park and the only remaining officer each took one of the two soldiers left alive by an arm. Together they jumped into the white waters. All were drowned.

One Negro in the party reached the riverbank alive. Isaaco, the faithful guide, learned the end of the story from him.

At the cost of nearly forty lives, Mungo Park had explored a stretch of the Niger unknown even to the Arab geographers. He had reached, though he did not know it, a point about 500 miles from the river's mouths. Where those mouths opened into the sea—or if they did—remained a mystery.

6. The Riddle Is Solved

The year was 1825. Twenty years had passed since Mungo Park's ill-fated journey. The course of the lower Niger was still a mystery, but more explorers were pursuing it, spurred by merchants eager for trade. Some geographers thought the Niger joined the Nile of Egypt. Others insisted that it flowed into the desert and disappeared through evaporation. Mungo Park had favored the idea that the Niger flowed into the Congo.

Now the British government hired a dashing young Scot named Hugh Clapperton to make another attempt at following the course of the Niger.

Richard Lander donned a turban and robe for this portrait which appeared in his first book about exploring the Niger.

To make the journey with him Clapperton hired a servant, a young man named Richard Lander. Lander had run away to sea at the age of eleven. His first journey was to the West Indies, as the servant of a merchant. In his mid-teens he traveled widely in Europe as a servant to various wealthy English families. Before he turned twenty, he had toured South Africa in the service of an English officer.

"There was a charm in the very sound of Africa that always made my heart flutter on hearing it mentioned," young Lander later confessed. So at the age of twenty-one he signed on with Hugh Clapperton.

Lander served Clapperton well as they traveled light-heartedly up through little-known kingdoms in what is now Nigeria. The young man could not, however, keep his master safe from the dread African fevers. In the spring of 1827 Hugh Clapperton died.

Many young men trained only to serve others would have panicked at being left alone in a strange land. Most would have headed for home as quickly as possible. Not Richard Lemon Lander!

He went on to visit Kano, a great trading city on the grasslands. Then he made his way through the

After Clapperton's death, Lander continued exploring along the Niger River, beginning at the grasslands city of Kano, below.

woods and farmlands of the Yoruba tribes, back to the coast, and from there to England. He took with him Clapperton's journal. When it was published in 1829, it was supplemented by "The Journal of Richard Lander from Kano to the Sea Coast."

Lander had shown such talents and abilities as an explorer that the British government soon sent him out on his own to discover the course of the lower Niger. This time he took along a younger brother, John, a printer by trade.

The Lander brothers reached the slave port of Badagri (not far from modern Lagos in Nigeria) in the spring of 1830. They followed the route that Richard Lander knew upcountry. They reached the Niger near Bussa Rapids, where Mungo Park's dream had ended.

The Landers continued up the riverbank for about 100 miles, asking wherever they could about the fate of Mungo Park. They were told the same story the guide Isaaco had reported earlier. At last they gave up that search, hired some canoes with Negro crews, and started downriver on their journey to the Niger's unknown mouth.

About 200 miles downriver from Bussa, the boats

The forest crowds in upon this typical Niger delta village.

came to a forking of the river. First they tried the left fork. The paddlers made little progress, because a strong current kept pushing them back. That current soon convinced the explorers that this river was not the Niger but another that flowed into it. It was actually the mighty Benue, the most important of the lower Niger's tributaries. Its name means "Mother of Waters."

Returning to the junction of the rivers, the little expedition continued on down the Niger. They soon found themselves surrounded by forests of tall mahogany, ebony, palm, and rubber trees that arched above the wide waters. Though the Landers did not realize it,

In Benin, not far from the Niger delta, sculptors of earlier days have left a record of the people and the animals of the area. The bronze figures of a leopard and a man blowing his horn were made in the 1600s and 1700s.

they were approaching the delta of the lower Niger.

The travelers had left behind the region of long-robed Moslems. They had left behind the grasslands with their memories of huge empires. Here there were not even middle-sized kingdoms like those the Landers had visited in the pleasant open country they had crossed on their way north.

In the rain forest there were no sacred kings. Groups living together had to be small, because food was hard to raise in the dense forest. Here vines, creepers, and high-crowned forest giants were so dense that roads had never been built. There were not even many trails on which a single line of men with headloads could march. Pack animals soon grew sick and died. The river and the mud-dark creeks were, therefore, the roads and highways of the rain forest. Dugout canoes were the only means of transport.

The men of each small family group—sons, brothers, and cousins—banded together to man a long war canoe. Each family that could support a sixty-man canoe had a voice in the government assembly. Government in the rain forest was thus quite democratic.

The principal crop of the forest was the thick, sweet,

starchy root called the yam. A man's wealth was measured by his yam crop. However, when Europeans found their way to the river mouths to trade, they, were not interested in yams. What the Europeans wanted to buy were slaves.

If their ships were not filled by the local traders, the slavers threatened to seize anyone they could reach. Partly to protect their own families, crews in war canoes soon began to go out on slaving raids through the forest creeks.

In the early 1800s the British were trying to stop the trade. There was still a market for slaves in the Americas, but the British had outlawed slavery.

At this time England was in the midst of the Industrial Revolution. Spinning and weaving and other crafts were being moved from small home workshops into factories with big machines.

These machines had to be oiled to keep them working smoothly. In the rain forests there were groves of palms whose fruit was rich in oil. Palm oil soon replaced slaving as the road to wealth. Delta men in their war canoes turned to fighting among themselves to control the palm oil trade.

Deep in the rain forest, a farmer, right, cuts the fruit from the palm tree. A village woman, below, extracts oil from the kernels of the fruit.

This drawing of a delta war canoe and warriors illustrated the book Richard Lander wrote about his second Niger expedition.

The Landers' party paddled into this country. It had just passed a very large open-air market when it encountered a fleet of fifty war canoes. The canoes flew a mixture of bright flags. Their crews sported some bright jackets and hats. Most important, each canoe had a big gun on its bow. Quickly the fleet sank one of the Landers' unarmed boats and boarded the other. The brothers and their crew were taken prisoner.

The Landers believed that they had been captured by

the king of the Ibos (*ee*-bows). Their captor was actually a local chief who wanted ransom. Richard Lander was certain that if he could just get to the coast and find an English ship, all would be well. Since he was on an expedition for the British government, surely any English captain would be glad to forward the ransom.

The delta chief thought that this sounded reasonable. Holding John Lander as a hostage, the chief sent Richard Lander under guard to the coast, where there was an English ship at anchor in the delta channel.

Thickets of mangrove, whose roots poke up above the water like lumpy knees, surround these delta river channels. The mangrove swamps continue for about seventy miles inland before firm banks replace the oozing mud, and true rain forest trees appear. Ocean-going ships can go fifteen to forty miles up these streams. On one of these streams Richard Lander found an English ship at anchor and went aboard.

There a shock awaited him. Most of the ship's crew were down with fever. This was not surprising. Lander had encountered plenty of fever in his travels. What shocked him was that the captain, after listening to his story, rudely swore that he would pay no ransom—

"not a flint!" Moreover, he said he would sail without the Landers if they could not win their own freedom.

What saved the two brothers was the illness of the English crew. The ship could not sail at once and leave the brothers there, as the captain had threatened. After some days, the palm-oil chieftain grew tired of waiting for the ransom and released both brothers. They boarded the ship, and at last it did make ready to sail. Yet danger still threatened.

At the mouth of the river, the ship had to clear the breakers of the open sea. At this point, the breeze died. The surf was running high. The ship rolled, nearly foundering in huge waves.

On shore, crews of the war canoes were waiting, expecting a wreck. Just in the nick of time, a breeze came up and filled the sails. This steadied the ship so that its longboat could tow it through the surf and out to safety. It is small wonder if for the moment the Landers forgot that they had really discovered where the Niger meets the sea!

7. The River's Last Secret

Like Mungo Park, Richard Lander found Africa a fatal lure. In 1832 he returned to Africa at the head of an expedition backed by English merchants. His plan was to open up trade on the Niger and to establish a base where the Benue flows into the main river.

As had happened so often to other expeditions, this one was hard hit by tropical fevers, diseases, and other troubles. In 1834 Richard Lander was wounded in a fight with local warriors on the river. He died of his wounds at the age of thirty.

No tales of death or disaster discouraged explorers of Africa. They kept coming to the land of the Niger from all directions. Many crossed the Sahara from the north. Some came overland from the Atlantic coast on the west. Others sailed to the Bight of Benin, the bay into which the mouths of the Niger empty. So many Europeans died in this area that sailors had a saying:

Beware, beware, the Bight of Benin!
One comes out where forty went in!

Still they came!

The British were busiest on the lower river. There they organized the Royal Niger Company to promote trade. They set up the Oil Rivers Protectorate to keep local tribes from fighting among themselves. They also sent expeditions far up the Benue and onto the grasslands.

While the British worked inland from the Niger delta, the French were pushing their way across country from the west. In the 1880s the nations of Western Europe divided Africa among themselves, completely disregarding tribes and turning once independent kingdoms into colonies. Belgians, British, Germans, Portuguese, and Spaniards took control of parts of the continent. The French took over most of West Africa.

The French followed the Senegal River up to the

A fisherman hangs up his nets to dry on the banks of the Niger River as in the days of French exploration.

high country. There they found not only the streams that fed the Senegal and Gambia rivers but other streams as well. It did not take the French long to discover that these other streams joined to form the Niger.

By 1883 the French had built forts on the Niger and had assembled a small gunboat on the river to protect the forts. French expeditions were also exploring and charting the various channels of the river.

Some of the explorers chopped their way through vines and thick brush to follow streams uphill. They passed villages made up of clusters of bamboo huts, each hut with its peaked roof of thatch. In the stream in front of the villages, men fished. Women and girls filled their water jugs and did their washing.

These forest people told the Frenchmen that, higher up in the green mountains, springs bubbled from the rocky slopes. The springs formed small pools, and, as the pools overflowed, the water ran away in sparkling streams. One such spring and its stream, the Tembi, were considered sacred. They were known as the Father or Source of the Joliba, as the Niger was called here.

In 1885 a French officer made his way to the spring of Tembi. With this visit the last mystery of the Niger was uncovered. Its source had been discovered.

8. Taming the River

There was still much to be learned about the Niger. Years passed before men completely charted the network of channels through delta mud—both in the inland delta and at the river's mouths.

The Niger gave up its secrets slowly, grudgingly. Its rocks and rapids battered the small boats of explorers. The sting of mosquitoes carried disease. Heat spoiled food supplies so that the explorers sickened and died. Still the pale-faced Europeans kept coming, dressed in their strange, heavy clothes.

Some of the strangers rode up and down the river in noisy boats that churned the waters. These steamboats were very different from the familiar canoes that slipped silently upstream or downstream while boatmen dipped their paddles smoothly and chanted or sang.

The strangers built walls of rock and earth to dam the river's flow, until waters piled up behind these walls in wide lakes. They even built bridges—one at Jebba in Nigeria—to carry railway trains across the Niger!

Strange new buildings went up in the cities along the riverbanks—forts and factories, covered markets and office buildings. The strangers brought in people to teach their language in new schools and their religion in new churches. They made Africans use European coins in trade.

Today some tribes are divided by the fact that part of their people have been taught to use French in schools and offices while the rest use English. Part of them have learned to buy and sell using French francs, while the others are familiar with English shillings.

After some years the French and the English thought that they had mastered the Niger and all the people who lived along its banks.

The French had dreams of developing the Niger valley, both as a great trade route across Africa and

In Mali, which the French once held, cotton is still grown near small villages. Above, a farmer examines his crop.

as an agricultural paradise. During the first half of the twentieth century, Frenchmen worked hard to make these dreams come true.

The French knew that the Niger rose in flood season like the Nile of Egypt. They knew that it, too, covered wide fields with rich mud. Local farmers had been growing two crops a year on these plots, with few tools except wooden hoes or pointed sticks. Their crops were generally millet (a hard grain), rice, and some cotton.

These children are playing in the flooded streets of a village in Niger, which was formerly a French colony.

Cotton was a once wild plant that had been cultivated in this area.

The French planned dams to control the flood waters, and canals to lead the water to more fields. They planned to introduce modern farming methods. They dreamed of limitless crops of rice and of cotton to rival those of Egypt and the United States.

The French did succeed in constructing a dam across the river at Sansanding. They also dug irrigation canals back from the river and set up stations to control river traffic. Somehow, despite all the French did, the great plan for transforming the Niger valley into a huge rice and cotton plantation did not succeed.

For one thing, the climate proved to be unsuited to growing very large crops of cotton. Another problem was the river itself. The change between the dry season and the time of flood is very great. During the dry months, water is very low in the main channel. In small pools of the channel, fish—trapped without plant life—often nearly starve. Then the flood sends the river over its banks and across the cotton fields. The high water releases the hungry fish, and they eat much of the young crop.

Another problem had to do with land ownership. Riverfront land was generally owned by rich and powerful families. Poorer people held drier inland plots. Irrigation projects promised to make these inland plots more fertile and valuable. However, dams that held back the river would make the water rise and flood riverfront lands. The owners of these front lands feared that too much water might harm their property. They objected to the irrigation plans.

In fact, all the farmers in the basin of the Niger liked their own way of growing crops. They did not want to change.

The French also dreamed of a great east-west route across the open grasslands. They planned for trade to go up the valley of the Senegal River by boat or rail, then by rail across to the Niger.

The railroad from the Atlantic coast should have connected with the river at Bamako, the first real city of the Niger after the river leaves the hills. A few miles below Bamako, however, rocks in the river channel make boat travel dangerous at low water. To avoid these rapids, the French built the railroad to Koulikoro, a town on the Niger about forty miles below the rapids.

The massive walls of the Kainji Dam, under construction on the Niger River, tower over two boatmen in a dugout canoe.

Transportation is still improving everywhere in the Niger basin. At this river crossing in Niger, a modern truck rolls off a ferry. Below, an airplane is readied for a takeoff at an airfield in Guinea.

Beyond Koulikoro a stretch of more than 1,000 miles of calm water is navigable by good-sized steamers. The French set up shipyards to build boats for this trade.

They also built roads and established an airline to connect the cities of French West Africa. Today the Niger basin is dotted with airports. Trains still make the 700-mile, 33-hour run between Dakar on the west coast and Koulikoro twice a week. Trucks roll over the roads between cities. Great modern trade routes have not yet developed, though, to compare with those the Niger knew under Mali and Songhai seven centuries or more ago.

9. A New Day Dawns

French and British power along the Niger lasted from the 1880s—or later—to the 1950s. This was a short period in the long history of civilization along the river. The king lists of the Songhai people alone stretch back over nearly 900 years.

By 1960 the lands of the Niger were once again ruled by men of the old, old African tribes. The French and British still tried to be friendly. The French pay part of the governmental expenses of lands they once ruled. Britain still has men acting as advisers to some officials in its former colonies. African leaders, however, are once again in control of their own countries.

The streams that feed the Niger rise in highlands that are now part of the nation of Guinea. The marshy grasslands where the Niger makes its great loop are now divided between two republics. One republic is named for the Mali empire of old. The other is called the Republic of Niger, in honor of the river itself.

Bamako on the upper Niger is now the capital of the Republic of Mali. It was the site that the French chose for one of their early forts, as they took control of the river and grasslands. Bamako was just a village when the French set up their colonial government about 1900. By the time independence came in 1958, it had grown to a city of more than 68,000.

With independence Bamako became the capital of the Sudanese Republic. After a brief period of union with Senegal, this republic broke away and changed its name, in 1960, to Mali.

The French fort of Bamako still overlooks the Niger from the top of a steep-sided hill. Today, however, its buildings are occupied by offices of the Mali government. Handsome white houses set in shady gardens in the city below are occupied by officials of Mali.

Trees planted by the French still shade many streets.

This citizen of Guinea voting in a presidential election is a symbol of the newly-attained independence of African nations.

European-made cars and motorcycles speed along the streets and across the French-built bridge over the Niger. Many signs in the city are printed in French. It is the flag of Mali, however, that flies over Bamako.

The Republic of Niger, another landlocked, largely desert country, adjoins Mali on the east. Its capital, Niamey, also stands on the banks of the river. It also has some blocks of white, French-style buildings with Arabic touches. Like Bamako, Niamey has an airport, and a bridge is being built over the river here. Most of the homes of Niamey—and of other Niger cities—are, however, of traditional African design.

An African home may be a neat cluster of round huts with walls of reeds or mud. It may be rectangular, built around an open central court. Usually one hut or room is for kitchen use. Near it is a grain storage bin with a raised doorsill to keep out animals. Another hut or room is for a wife, her unmarried daughters, and her small sons to sleep in. Each grown man in the family has his own sleeping hut. The living room is out of doors, and most of the cooking is done there, on a hearth of three stones.

The West African housewife does most of her marketing at open-air stalls. The main market of the town is often near the river, as in Timbuktu. Here mounds of watermelons, trays of peanuts, dates, and kola nuts are on display. There are heaps of grain and stacks of dried fish for sale. There are also bundles of twisty thornbush firewood and other bundles of reeds for thatching roofs or weaving floor mats.

Craftsmen are at work not far away. Tuaregs pound spears and daggers into shape in out-of-door shops

In this village market near Niamey, a salesman offers boat-men's poles for sale.

under the thin shade of thorn trees. They heat the metal in fires kept aglow by small boys pushing at goatskin bellows. Their women, sitting on grass mats, stitch leather bags and amulet cases to hold lucky charms.

Weavers sit at narrow looms making long ribbons of cloth to be sewed together into robes. In this part of Africa men generally do the weaving; women, the spinning of thread.

Hairdressers, seated on the ground with their customers stretched out in front of them, braid ladies' black locks into pigtails. Water carriers saunter past with goatskins of water on their heads, and porters shout as they load or unload bales of grain or fodder.

Livestock is sold near the water. Small horses and donkeys stand there quietly. Camels are hobbled near bushes they can nibble, and pens enclose sheep and goats.

Timbuktu's central marketplace is now surrounded by brick buildings built by the French. In the dim shops around the square, shelves are stacked with imported goods. There are blankets, sheets, cotton yard

In the busy city of Bamako, goods are sold in a covered market.

goods, soap, toothpaste, hair oil, and soft drinks. Most of the merchants who own these shops live above them, as in the old days.

In the center of the open square, market women sit under straw parasols. They offer for sale gourds of milk, a few eggs, stacks of dried fish, handfuls of kola nuts, lumps of charcoal, and trays of jewelry made of woven straw and wax. To go into business in a market like this does not take much of an investment.

Until a few years ago the riverfront market, said to be the largest and busiest on the Niger, and perhaps in all Africa, was in Onitsha, 150 miles or so inland from the mouths of the Niger. Every day scores of long canoes and bamboo-roofed houseboats arrived at Onitsha. They brought fish, yams, beans, millet, rice, onions, and other crops. In addition to the busy out-of-door market, there were neat rows of clean, modern, concrete market buildings.

Onitsha was a lively city of the Eastern Region of Nigeria. This basin of the lower Niger had been part of the British protectorate or colony of Nigeria for some years. After Nigeria became independent of Great Britain in 1960, it became a federation of several divi-

Market women offer their wares on large platters in the open square of a Nigerian village.

sions called regions. These were the Northern, Western, and Eastern Regions. Later, a Midwestern Region was created.

The new nation was troubled with rivalries among these regions, and among tribal peoples. It happened that the missionaries had given people of the Eastern Region a headstart in modern education. When Nigeria became self-governing, many of these well-educated men from the Eastern Region went to work in government offices in the Northern and Western regions. This led to jealousy, and as a result of this and other problems, many Eastern Nigerians were driven out of other parts of the country or killed.

The men of the Eastern Region had sat in their own governing assemblies a hundred years ago. Their region had most of Nigeria's industries, including coal mining and oil production. They decided that they could get along better by themselves than in the federation. Therefore they broke away from Nigeria in 1967 and set up a nation of their own, called Biafra.

Nigeria would not accept this. Its leaders sent the federal army to force Biafra to return to the union. Biafrans tried to fight for their independence, but they could not buy enough guns and planes to fight the Nigerian army. Most other countries did not like to see a new nation split in two, so Biafra got little outside help. It could not grow enough food to feed its people, and Nigeria would not let supplies enter Biafra. At last in 1970 Biafra had to give up and return to Nigeria, but not before hundreds of thousands of its people had suffered and starved and died.

At the war's end many of the cities and villages of the delta and the rain forest lay in ruins. Factories had crumbled. The once busy market towns like Onitsha were sad ghosts of their old selves. But these were stubborn ghosts. They soon began stirring back to life. The life force of the Niger, it seems, cannot be conquered.

Come what may, the rains pour down on the highlands, and the swollen waters make their way toward the distant sea. Fish spawn among the reeds, feed on water plants, and are finally hauled wriggling into the nets or gourds of fishermen. The fishermen then thank the spirit of the river for their catch.

In the north, herdsmen lead their wide-horned cattle and their sheep and goats down to the waters to drink.

Along hundreds of miles of river, farmers clear plots by burning off grass and brush with smudges of smoky fire. They plant and tend their crops. When the harvests are in, they give thanks to the spirits and carry their crops to market.

Canoes glide along the river channels with loads of grain, rice, and iron topped with kola nuts and perhaps some straw hats and calabash bowls.

Families ride from town to town on steamers, cooking their meals and sleeping on the shaded deck. When the steamer approaches a town, market women wade into the river holding up bowls of milk, loaves of bread, dried fish, and live chickens. The women of the traveling families can do their shopping without going ashore.

Prayer calls still ring out from the minarets of the mosques in grassland towns. In delta towns the spires of Christian churches rise, sometimes as tall as trees of the rain forest. The older religion of the Niger basin lives on, though, in countless hearts. It teaches that every object, every thing in nature has a spirit, a soul. When the people celebrate, they invite the spirits to join them—the spirits of their ancestors, the spirits of the antelope they hunt, of the crocodile that sometimes

As in centuries gone by, starting a journey down the Niger is a time for good-byes.

makes fishing dangerous, the spirit of the Niger River itself.

When it is time for feasting, the spirit guests are offered food first. In the plays and dances, the spirits are represented by men in carved masks. Music and dancing are planned to give pleasure to the people, but also to keep the spirits friendly. Living in harmony with nature, with one another, and with the world of spirits seems more important than having modern factories and electrical gadgets.

In Mopti, Moslems worship at a mosque, above, and dancers, left, celebrate a festival of the animist, or spirit, religion.

People from these grasslands and woodlands took some of their beliefs and traditions with them as they moved, many years ago, across Africa or across the Atlantic. Glimpses of ways of living in lands along the Niger, therefore, do more than introduce some of the new West African nations and the history that lies behind them. These glimpses can also help us to appreciate the rich background of Negro people who live in many other lands today. Hundreds, even thousands of miles from the wide valley where the "Nile of the Negroes" flows in its long, curving path to the sea, something of the spirit of the Niger lives on.

Picture credits:

Index

Meet the Author

JANE WERNER WATSON has written, edited, and compiled more than 200 books for young people from picture book age to the teens in a subject range which is encyclopedic. Mrs. Watson and her husband have traveled extensively in more than 65 countries of the world recording their travels with photographs, many of which appear in her books.

On two trips to Africa the Watsons have explored the rain forests, pleasant wooded farmlands of the savanna, and the dry thornbush country of the sub-Sahara nations. They have flown over sand-pale cities like ancient Gao and strolled the banks of the Niger in Bamako and Niamey. A deep interest in history has led them to further exploration through reading about the great kingdoms of Africa's past.

Mrs. Watson brings a rich store of information and firsthand experience, as well as an ability to present facts in a lively and interesting way, to this book about Africa's river of mystery.